GERMAN HIGHER EDUCATION: ISSUES AND CHALLENGES

by Hans G. Lingens

Phi Delta Kappa
International Studies in Education

We can only see in a picture what our experience permits us to see.

Edgar Dale

The Phi Delta Kappa International Studies in Education Series was established as a way to enlarge the common experience of education by publishing studies that bring to readers knowledge of heretofore unfamiliar theories, philosophies, and practices in the profession of education.

As the interdependence of nations becomes increasingly evident and necessary with the passage of time, so too must our understandings about education become shared property. In thus sharing, we come increasingly to comprehend one another across civilizations and cultures, for education is at the core of human endeavor. Through education we pass on to succeeding generations not merely the accumulated wisdom of our past but the vision and means to create the future.

German Higher Education: Issues and Challenges is the fifth monograph in this series.

Previous titles:
Elementary Teacher Education in Korea
Teacher Education in the People's Republic of China
Innovation in Russian Schools
Changing Traditions in Germany's Public Schools

INTERNATIONAL STUDIES
IN EDUCATION

GERMAN HIGHER EDUCATION: ISSUES AND CHALLENGES

by Hans G. Lingens

PHI DELTA KAPPA
EDUCATIONAL FOUNDATION
Bloomington, Indiana
U.S.A.

Cover design by
Peg Caudell

Library of Congress Catalog Card Number 97-75466
ISBN 0-87367-397-2
Copyright © 1998 by Hans G. Lingens
Bloomington, Indiana U.S.A.

To my wife,
Barbara-Jean Lingens

TABLE OF CONTENTS

INTRODUCTION

Germany is a country of contrasts. Great achievements in science, technology, the humanities, music, religion, and economics stand in stark opposition to disastrous politics, wars, and the elimination of more than six million people. A country with few natural resources, it competes successfully with the United States in world trade and technology.

What makes this nation so successful? How did Germany grow out of complete collapse into one of the leading economic powers in the world? The answer lies in the willingness of its people to build, to sacrifice for the common good, to adjust to an ever-changing world, to plan for the future, to keep on learning, and most important, to educate their young.

In Germany education is not left only to the schools. Education is everyone's business. Parents, communities, politicians, businesses, and industry all are deeply involved. There is no one education system in Germany; instead, there are many diverse systems.

It is important to look beyond our borders and to learn from others. Studying education systems in foreign countries helps us to gain a better understanding of education and policy development at home. We can reflect on our own system and see that our problems and concerns are not unique.

An education system also must be understood within its social, economic, and political setting. As societies are different, so are their education systems.

The higher education system in Germany produces excellent professionals while having to deal with many problems. For example, the number of students is increasing beyond the capacity of the

1

institutions to accommodate them. In addition, the nation's social structure is changing, partly because of the reunification of Germany and the formation of the European Community.

This monograph outlines some of the problems faced by higher education in Germany. The first chapter briefly describes the development of higher education and the changes in this system over time. Emphasis is placed on the development of higher education in the two Germanys before reunification, with some comments on developments since reunification.

Chapter 2 is divided into two parts. The first describes the various institutions, their mission and goals, concentrating especially on the universities and the colleges for higher professional training (*Fachhochschulen*). The second part is concerned with research, where it is conducted and who supports it.

Chapter 3 examines issues related to the administration and finance of higher education in Germany. It includes a discussion of some of the political circumstances that are a source of tension between the education institutions and the federal and state governments.

Chapter 4 focuses on the students. In addition to a general description of student characteristics, this chapter also discusses admission requirements, courses of study, financial aid, and the prospects for employment after graduation.

Teacher education programs in Germany are the subject of Chapter 5. German teacher education is known for being thorough and highly academic, but new conditions caused by the European Union are certain to cause changes in the system.

Finally, Chapter 6 examines some of the major issues that still need to be resolved. A variety of reforms already have been proposed for German higher education, and further reforms probably will be necessary to meet new conditions in the European Union.

CHAPTER ONE
A HISTORICAL SKETCH

Higher education in Germany has its origin in the schools attached to monasteries and churches in the Middle Ages. Access to those schools was limited to the nobility and those who were being trained for the clergy, and the teaching was dictated by the dogmas and beliefs of the church.

The first universities founded in the Germanic territories of Europe were the universities of Prague (1348), Vienna (1365), and Heidelberg (1386). Many other universities were founded by local rulers from 1300 to 1500. Following the tradition set at the universities of Bologna (1215) and Paris (1219), these universities were largely permitted to manage their own affairs. But their main purpose still was to educate the clergy and state servants.

In the early 19th century, Wilhelm von Humboldt (1767-1835) proposed major changes in the purposes of German universities. When the University of Berlin was founded in 1810, Humboldt asserted that the university should promote both teaching and basic research, because teaching needs to come out of research. In addition, he argued, the university should be autonomous with respect to research and teaching, and thus it must be independent of political, religious, or financial constraints (Brubacher and Rudy 1968). Two concepts were considered necessary to maintain that autonomy: *Lehrfreiheit* (freedom to teach), which meant that the professor has the freedom to explore all problems in his research and to teach and publish his findings without any impediments; and *Lernfreiheit* (freedom to learn), which meant that a student can take any course he or she chooses without formal attendance requirements or examinations until the final degree examination (Brubacher and Rudy 1968). The goal was to guarantee the best training so that the graduate could think independently in professional life and in society (Preisert and Framhein 1994).

New methods of instruction were introduced, such as the seminar, the specialist's lecture, the laboratory, and the training of specialist or professional faculties. Rote learning was replaced by independent learning, and students participated in research. The universities added more areas of study over time, but this original structure and governance of the university remained until the 1970s.

In the last half of the 19th century, technical and polytechnic schools developed into technical universities (*Technische Hochschulen*) and concentrated on engineering and sciences. In the early 20th century, teacher training academies (*Pädagogische Akademien*) were formed to train primary school (*Grundschule*) and what now are called main school (*Hauptschule*) teachers. These universities had great difficulty achieving the same status as the traditional universities. Indeed, in most states they eventually became part of the traditional universities and ceased to exist independently.

Even though they were state institutions, the traditional universities remained largely autonomous. The chaired professors (*Ordinarien*) ruled on all academic and administrative matters. In fact, it was not uncommon for a chaired professor to ask for and receive an institute that was built to his specification. However, the universities had to struggle to maintain their political independence throughout their history. For example, after the founding of Imperial Germany in 1871, the government saw the purpose of the universities as serving the state by providing highly educated civil servants.

The greatest challenge for the German universities came from the Nazi dictatorship from 1933 to 1945. The Reich's Ministry of Science, Education, and Popular Education strictly controlled every aspect of the universities. Many professors and students were banned from the universities because they were Jewish or believed in democratic principles, and many professors left Germany to avoid persecution. At some universities, up to one-third of the faculty was lost. The number of students dropped dramatically from 121,000 in 1933 to 56,000 in 1938. In addition, research and teaching were greatly harmed by the loss of many scientists and the destruction of facilities during the war (Preisert and Framhein 1994).

The German Democratic Republic

After World War II the German Democratic Republic (GDR or, in German, Deutsche Demokratische Republik, DDR) and the Federal Republic of Germany (FRG, or Bundesrepublik Deutschland, BDR) developed separate education systems that matched their political structures. Higher education in the GDR was structured according to Marxist-Leninist ideology. It was centrally planned and controlled in order to train professionals for the centrally planned and controlled economy. Academic freedom was greatly curtailed, and Marxism-Leninism was an important part of the curriculum. The universities lost their autonomy; and examinations, course length, and curricula were controlled by the government.

University governance also changed. The traditional faculties and institutes were dissolved and replaced with sections. In addition, a socialist council and an academic council were appointed to support the rector, who was the chief administrator. Both councils were advisory and were dominated by party members and members of the Communist youth organization.

The East German government opened higher education to the children of workers and peasants. To make this access as broad as possible, the universities provided correspondence courses so that workers could study without taking time off from their jobs. The only entrance requirement for these students was to possess the *Abitur* (secondary leaving certificate), which meant that the student had passed the comprehensive graduation examination at the conclusion of his or her secondary school education in a traditional *Gymnasium* (college-prep high school).

The number of students grew quickly until 1970, when there were about 100,000 regular university students and 40,000 correspondence and evening students (Preisert and Framhein 1994). This represented about 17% of the college-age people in the GDR. However, the government began to limit admissions in the 1970s in order to meet its plans for the manpower needs of industry and commerce. During those years, only 30,000 students were admitted each year in order to keep the overall student population at 130,000.

To be admitted to a university, a student needed the Abitur as a start. But the student then had to undergo an ideological and placement screening to determine his or her commitment to contributing to a socialist society, as well as where the candidate could best meet society's needs (Max-Planck-Institute 1994).

Higher education and research in the GDR were subordinated to the planned economy. Institutions of higher learning were charged mainly with teaching and political indoctrination. Most research took place in academies separate from universities. Research academies were under even tighter central control and employed only individuals with strong party loyalty. Industry, which also was controlled by the government, influenced research; and some universities and research institutions were tied directly to industrial enterprises, especially in the areas of mechanical engineering and scientific instrumentation. Basic research, on the other hand, was not heavily supported, because it did not have immediate application in industry, commerce, or society (Preisert and Framhein 1994).

In general, university offerings were limited in East Germany. In the technical fields, course offerings were narrowly tailored to the needs of the regime and the economy (*Perspectiven für Wissenschaft* 1990). Research in the social studies and humanities was not important to the regime.

The Federal Republic of Germany

In the Federal Republic of Germany after World War II, higher education expanded and the ideals of Wilhelm von Humboldt were once again enforced. It was a monumental task just to rebuild

8

the universities, many of which rose like a phoenix from the charred rubble. But internal renewal was even more important. Some professors returned from exile; but others had to undergo the de-Nazification process and could return to their profession only when they were considered employable.

When the Federal Republic of Germany was established in 1949, the states were given complete authority in education and culture; the federal government could not interfere. Rebuilding universities and other institutions of learning thus was the responsibility of the ministries of culture and education in the individual states. However, politicians and educators feared that a differing quality of education in the states would bring economic progress to a halt. Many issues pertaining to education and training needed to be resolved on a nationwide basis. Examinations and professional qualifications had to be acknowledged throughout Germany. For that reason, some nationwide agreements on educational processes and content of instruction had to be reached. The first agency created to ensure that the federal government and the states could work together was the Science Council (*Wissenschaftsrat*), formed in 1957. The Science Council made nonbinding recommendations to the various government agencies for educational development. Other national organizations included the Standing Conference of the Ministers of Education of the States (*Ständige Konferenz der Kultusminister der Länder in der Bundesrepublik Deutschland, KMK*) and the West German Rectors Conference (*Westdeutsche Rektorenkonferenz, WRK*). Both agencies worked to harmonize education throughout the Federal Republic.

Development and expansion of higher education was of great concern. Before the Second World War, Germany had 24 universities and 14 technical universities. Of those, 16 universities and nine technical universities were located in the territory that became West Germany. There are now more than 250 institutions of higher learning in the West German states.

The number of students in the FRG increased steadily after the war, and the number doubled in the 1950s (*Stifterverband für die Deutsche Wissenschaft*, 1993). Not only did the system have diffi-

9

culty absorbing the increased number of students, but many of those students were not part of the intellectual elite who traditionally attended the universities. The universities still operated as institutions for elite students, and teaching and research were conducted with little concern for practicality. It still was assumed that students would be able to acquire their professional qualifications without formal programs.

In 1969, new institutions of higher education, the colleges of higher professional training (*Fachhochschulen*), were established to meet the need for expansion. These colleges originated in the former engineering schools and specialized technical colleges. Another institution formed to meet the increase in the number of students was the amalgamated university (*Gesamthochschule*). This institution incorporates offerings from the university, college of education, and Fachhochschule in an interdisciplinary approach. Students at an amalgamated university can direct their studies toward a variety of degrees.

The university governance structure also changed from one that was authoritarian to one that is more democratic and participatory. The traditional large faculties (*Fakultäten*) were replaced by smaller departments that include broader areas. In addition, the administration no longer was the privilege exclusively of the chaired professors (*Ordinarien*). Instead, the administration included all employees. Other changes included shortening the time required for various kinds of study.

One major change in university governance is the result of the Federal Framework Act for Higher Education of the Federal Republic, which took effect in 1976. Under this law, the federal government provides a uniform legal framework for all institutions of higher learning. The law allows enough leeway for regional and state differences, but the states have had to adjust their own education laws to fit into the federal framework. In this way, the federal government has become more formally involved in planning, financing, and building institutions for higher education. In addition, the federal government also became responsible for the financial support of students.

Because it was difficult for universities to accommodate the ever-increasing number of students, the admission process for new students came under debate. One proposal was to limit access; however, in 1977 the heads of the federal and state governments decided not to restrict admission to higher education. Thus all institutions of higher learning became overcrowded, and they have stayed overcrowded ever since. By 1993, including the institutions in the former East Germany, about 1.8 million students were registered in higher education, twice the capacity that can be accommodated easily.

Reunification

Political reunification of the GDR and FRG was officially completed in 1990. However, much work still needed to be done to bring the two systems together. A joint commission for education was formed to create a uniform approach to higher education throughout Germany. The institutions of the former GDR were integrated into the organizations and committees of the FRG as equal members. Thus the East German higher education institutions are represented in the Science Council (*Wissenschaftsrat*), the Higher Education Rectors Conference (*Hochschulrektorenkonferenz*), the Federal-States Commission for Educational Planning (*Bund-Länder Komission für Bildungsplanung und Forschungsförderung*), the Planning Committee for Higher Education Building (*Planungausschuß für den Hochschulbau*), the Conference of the Ministers of Education and Cultural Affairs (*Kultusministerkonferenz, KMK*), and several others.

In particular, since 1990 the Science Council, which now included academics from the new states, recommended restructuring research and teaching in the former GDR according to the West German model. Since then, more than 1,000 research academies have been reorganized and integrated into the higher education system to strengthen the research and teaching function of the universities. Fachhochschulen also were established at this time. The FRG provided large sums of money to support these efforts. In addition, each of the new states had to develop its own higher education legislation within the Federal Framework Act for Higher Education of the Federal Republic so that it could benefit from cooperation.

Many observers believe that the accession of the new states has provided a chance to reform higher education in all of Germany, not just in the former German Democratic Republic. Some attempts are being made to do so. However, several traditional aspects of the university system interfere with new ideas. Innovators must face the difficult challenge of convincing policy makers and the general public that modernization is necessary to meet the changes in Germany's economy and social structure.

CHAPTER TWO

TYPES OF INSTITUTIONS AND
RESEARCH SOCIETIES

German institutions of higher education include universities and technical universities, colleges of education for teacher training, colleges of art and music, colleges for higher professional training (*Fachhochschulen*), amalgamated universities (*Gesamthochschulen*), distance-learning universities, and professional academies (*Berufsakademien*).

There are more than 300 such institutions in united Germany's 16 states. These institutions show great diversity, not only from state to state but also within a given state and among the same kind of institutions. However, their diplomas or other final examinations are recognized and accepted in all of Germany and beyond. The Framework Act for Higher Education ensures some uniformity among institutions, and certain other commonalities result from tradition.

Universities and Technical Universities

The most traditional institutions are the universities and the technical universities, and they provide the standards by which higher education is measured. The goal of most students is to attend a traditional university, and this sector of higher education still has the largest number of students.

The purpose of the universities is to develop scientific exploration in all disciplines (*Entwicklung der Wissenschaften*) through research and teaching (*Framework Act for Higher Education*, 1994). Ideally, this purpose should be accomplished without regard for practical applications; the only guide for teaching and research should be the need to know. Indeed, the freedom of art and science, research, teaching, and study is guaranteed under the Basic Law (*Grundgesetz*), which is the German constitution. However, practicality dictates that these studies also must prepare students for various occupations.

Of all the institutions in higher education, the universities offer the broadest spectrum of subjects for study and research. The broad subject fields offered at universities include economics, law, theology, social sciences, natural sciences, philosophy, agricultural science, engineering, and medicine. Of course, not all subjects receive the same emphasis at all universities. A few universities concentrate on certain fields of study or are known for special areas of concentration. For example, the armed forces have two universities for training future officers. Some universities specialize in veterinary medicine, administration, economics, and sports.

Technical universities originally were restricted to engineering and the natural sciences, and they were not considered equal to the traditional university. However, the increasing demand for higher education has caused policy makers to include other disciplines in the technical universities and to bring them to full university status.

In addition to the chaired professors, a university faculty consists of temporary and part-time employees, including nonchaired professors (*Privatedozente*), temporary professors (*Außerplanmäßige Professoren*), lecturers (*Lehrbeauftragte*), and teaching and research assistants at various levels (*wissenschaftliche Hilfskräfte*). In addition, there is a full-time civil service staff.

Except for engineering and medicine, the courses of study at the universities are not tightly organized. Studies consist of basic or general studies (*Grundstudium*) for four semesters in a chosen field, then main studies (*Hauptstudium*) with areas of concentration, which also have a suggested length of four semesters.

Before being admitted to the main studies, a student has to pass an interim examination. The main studies allow for in-depth exploration and specialization in a given field. The student has to take mandatory courses, courses from a series of obligatory electives, and other electives for further specialization.

There are special prerequisites for some areas of study. For example, a knowledge of Latin is required to study history, foreign languages, religion, philosophy, theology, and law; and in some instances Latin is required for a master's degree. Also, students who wish to study engineering are required to engage in a practicum beforehand. The regulations concerning prerequisites differ among the states, and sometimes they are different from one university to the next within a state.

To earn a diploma in the natural sciences, engineering, business, and social sciences, students must pass an exam. The diploma certifies that the student has specialized in one area of studies or in one subject. The other courses the student has taken must relate to the main emphasis of the diploma. For example, a student who specializes in urban architecture might take other courses in architecture.

In language, humanities, some areas of social studies, and the natural sciences, the final examination qualifies the student for a master's degree (*Magister*). For this degree, the student can major in one subject and also select two minor subjects. Or the student can elect to major in two subjects that are independent of one another.

The diploma and the master's degree are awarded through examinations administered by the university. On the other hand, studies in medicine, veterinary medicine, dentistry, pharmacy, food sciences, law, and teaching end with examinations administered by the state. In addition, teaching and law require students to engage in a practicum as part of or closely following their formal studies; and following the practicum, students must pass a second state examination before they can formally enter their profession. (Churches give similar examinations in theology before aspiring ministers can enter their seminaries.) Such examinations usually include a major research paper in the chosen area of concentration and an oral or written examination.

Except for a few experimental programs, there are no formal doctoral programs. Instead, the doctoral student is guided by an advisor or sponsor (*Doktor Vater*, literally "doctor father") and usually works independently. Preparing a dissertation can take several years, during which the student works at the university or in subject-related employment. Medical students can prepare their dissertation during their studies. After the dissertation has been accepted, the candidate has to defend the findings in an oral examination.

Colleges for Higher Professional Training

After World War II, the German economy had an increasing need for highly skilled professionals. Industry and commerce needed people who had focused and practical knowledge that was applicable to day-to-day operations.

To respond to these needs, a new institution of higher education, the college for higher professional training (*Fachhochschule*), was established around 1970. There were 132 Fachhochschulen in 1994, and more are planned.

The mandate of the Fachhochschule is to provide practical courses and research. Their study offerings include engineering, business, agriculture, social work, design and form, library science, information science, and public administration. Currently the subject offerings at Fachhochschulen are expanding. For example, originally law was taught exclusively at universities, but economic law now is taught at some Fachhochschulen.

Some Fachhochschulen are specialized in their offerings. For example, there are Fachhochschulen for public administration where only persons already employed in the civil service can enroll. Others are sponsored by churches, especially Fachhochschulen for social services.

The staffing at Fachhochschulen is similar to that at universities. Professors need to show appropriate qualifications and to have finished a course of study in higher education combined with research. Usually this is accomplished by holding an advanced degree or through special qualifications in the arts. In the Fachhochschule, however, more emphasis is placed on ability to teach than on research. Professors at Fachhochschulen also need to have five years of practical experience with at least three years outside of higher education. They teach up to 18 hours a week, which can be reduced for research purposes. In some states the professors are able to take a semester leave of absence, usually every four years, to work in their profession and update their practical knowledge.

In contrast to the loosely articulated majors at the universities, there is a definite structure to the course of study at Fachhochschulen. Teaching and learning is more formal and focused on professional abilities, rather than on theoretical knowledge.

While the course of study varies among the states, it usually lasts four years, including a semester or two in a practicum. Students also must participate in a practicum before being admitted to the school. However, if the student has worked in a job related to the course of study, the pre-admission practicum can be waived. And if the student can show proof of having successfully finished training in the area of study before entering, he or she can have one of the semesters of practicum waived. To graduate, the student must pass a rigorous examination.

Some Fachhochschulen work cooperatively with industry and combine in-plant training with theoretical studies. Students in these schools take two examinations, one administered by the Chamber of Industry and Commerce and one administered by the Fachhochschule.

The students who graduate from the Fachhochschule receive a diploma designating their area of expertise. At one time, the designation "FH" (Fachhochschule) was added to the diploma to differentiate it from a university diploma. However, in recent years this requirement has been dropped; and in most places, the diplomas of both the Fachhochschulen and the universities are considered equal.

Distance Universities

The Distance University (*Fernuniversität*) in Hagen also is an amalgamated university and offers courses for academic credits.

The courses, offered on both a full-time and part-time basis, can lead to a diploma or master's degree. Students must take examinations to graduate, as in regular universities.

Study centers for this university can be found in several cities in Germany, Austria, Switzerland, and Hungary. These centers are staffed by mentors and offer counseling and testing. In addition, students can fulfill residency requirements at the study centers. For handicapped students, home visits can be arranged and, under the supervision of a representative of the university, examinations can be taken at home.

The Fernuniversität was the only university in the West German states to offer distance learning. Now some universities in the new states of the former East Germany also offer distance courses through written and audiovisual media. Some Fachhochschulen in the new states also offer a wide range of courses with a combination of distance and residence studies, especially in information sciences, mechanical engineering, electrical engineering, and business administration. The general public can take courses without formal enrollment in higher education; but no one can achieve a degree without formal admission to higher education.

Some universities also cater to working people with learning programs that aid in their work, such as business administration and business engineering. The Science Council and the Federal-States Commission for Educational Planning and Research Promotion have recommended expanding this option, especially because of the need to stay competitive in the European Union.

Special Institutions

Another type of institution, the college of education (*Pädagogische Hochschule*), developed after World War II. These institutions were concerned mainly with teacher training for primary schools (*Grundschulen*), main schools (*Hauptschulen*), special schools (*Sonderschulen*), and sometimes for the middle schools (*Realschulen*) and secondary level one (*Sekundarstufe I*). Most colleges of education were integrated into the universities in the

1960s and 1970s or were upgraded to universities with the full spectrum of university offerings. Only a few are still independent.

Special institutions also developed for the arts (*Kunsthochschulen*) and music (*Musikhochschulen*). These tend to be relatively small schools. Their emphasis is on developing individual talents in small-group or individual sessions. Generally, studies are not structured and do not require an examination at the end. However, a course of study can end in a final examination and an artistic degree, such as master student or a diploma. In addition, students at these schools can study to be art and music teachers, occupations that require a state examination followed by a practical induction into teaching.

Another institution of higher education is the amalgamated, or comprehensive, university (*Gesamthochschule*). This type of university came into existence about 1970 in an effort to combine the research and teaching done by universities, colleges of education, Fachhochschulen, and the music and arts colleges. However, the idea did not take hold very firmly, and today only a few of these institutions exist in the states of North Rhine-Westphalia and Hesse. The Gesamthochschulen offer two different types of degrees. One is similar to the university degree, and the other is similar to the degree offered by the Fachhochschulen.

The professional academies (*Berufsakademien*) are another new and special form of higher education. The first ones were established in 1974, and there still are only a few of them. The Berufsakademien provide students with both theoretical and practical training for their chosen profession. Areas of training include economics, technical areas, and sociology. Berufsakademien are connected to the state system, but they are located at the training facilities of certain industries.

To enroll in a professional academy, the student must have finished an apprenticeship or training with an affiliated business or industry, in addition to having the Abitur or similar qualification for higher education. Training alternates every three months between the academy and workplace. After two years and a final examination, the student can achieve an assistantship; and after three years and an examination, the student can receive a diploma as manager, engineer, or social service professional (*Sozialpädagoge*). The examination is equivalent to the final examination of the Fachhochschulen.

Germany also has 62 private institutions of higher education, with a total student population of 30,000. They have full recognition and award degrees and diplomas. Among the courses offered by private universities are medicine, dentistry, economics, and art and design. Private institutions charge tuition.

Churches and religious communities also run higher education institutions, offering studies in theology, philosophy, social science, and other subjects close to the churches. Churches also operate their own training institutions for priests and ministers, supplementing the theological training of universities. Among the church-run institutions are 17 Fachhochschulen for social work.

Research

The German economy depends heavily on basic and applied research to find quick solutions to problems and to remain competitive in the global market. Germany spends 3% of its gross national product (GNP) on research and development (compared to 2.7% in Japan and 2.8% in the United States). The German economy depends heavily on its export of technology-dependent goods, and German industry values research highly.

Traditionally, basic research is conducted at universities and technical universities. Indeed, research is seen to be inseparable from teaching. University professors are expected to do research, and they are guaranteed the freedom to choose their research domain.

One condition for German reunification was the realignment of the research structure in East Germany. In the former German Democratic Republic, research was done in special research academies; universities were charged only with teaching. After unification, research was transferred back to the universities to fulfill the constitutional mandate that both teaching and research be conducted in higher education institutions. The 1,300 qualified scientists of the former research academies were offered positions in the new higher education structure under a specially funded, limited-time, federal program. This program is about to be terminated for lack of funds, and scientists who have not been placed will have to be absorbed into other programs or face unemployment ("Hochschulen: Letzte Hoffnung," 1996).

Although teaching and research commonly are seen as closely linked, research institutions have been established that are independent of higher education. Their purpose is to provide the flexibility in research and development that is needed by industry. Although these institutions are independent, they do cooperate with each other and with higher education on a continual basis through formal meetings. These meetings include the Higher Education Rectors Conference and the Science Council.

These research institutions can be divided into three groups. The first includes large-scale research centers and the Max Planck Society Institutes. These deal mainly with basic research. A second group works in applied research and includes the Fraunhof Society Institutes. A third group is charged with research projects with supraregional importance, such as distance learning. These institutions include the Blue List Institutions.

The German Society for Promotion of Research (*Deutsche Forschungsgemeinschaft*) is an autonomous organization that promotes science at higher education institutions, scientific academies, independent research institutions, and scientific associations. Any researcher can apply for financial assistance for any proposed project, and projects can be financed for up to 15 years. Project evaluation committees are staffed by volunteers elected every four years. Every scientist who has had a doctoral degree for at least three years can vote. The society advises parliament and represents German research at international levels. Federal ministries provide support; and the federal and state governments fund the budget, which was DM 1.5 billion in 1993.

The Max Planck Society (*Max Planck Gesellschaft*) promotes basic research and supplements research conducted at universities. It has 65 institutes and 27 working groups in the new states. The society concentrates on three research areas: bio-medical, chemical-physical-technical, and the humanities. The society is concerned with international cooperation and employs many foreign nationals as directors and guest scientists (Max-Planck-Gesellschaft 1996).

Anyone willing to promote science and research can join this nonprofit society, which has 11,050 members, including 3,050 researchers. In 1993, stipends were given to 5,500 guest scientists and doctoral candidates. The Max Planck Society's budget is provided by the federal government, the states, and industry. In 1994, the proposed budget was DM 1.6 billion, of which DM 1.5 billion came from government sources.

The Association of Large Research Institutions (*Arbeitsgemeinschaft der Großforschungseinrichtungen*) has 16 large research centers and 23,000 members, of which 11,000 are scientists. One of its major efforts is to coordinate research and technical development, especially in the natural sciences, engineering, and biomedical research. The Federal Ministry of Education and Research provides major funding (DM 3 billion in 1993). University professors are usually in decision-making positions. The association employs young scientists for up to three years, and about 1,000 doctoral candidates work in its research centers. This society also promotes international cooperation and employs about 700 scientists from other countries.

The Fraunhof Society for the Promotion of Applied Research (*Fraunhofer Gesellschaft*) is concerned with applied research. The society works under the commission of industry, government, other public enterprises, and the European Union. Heavy emphasis is placed on environmental research, new energy sources, and safety of technical equipment. The society has 47 centers throughout Germany. Some centers are directly associated with higher education institutions, others are affiliated with industry. The society is expanding worldwide, with centers in Europe, the United States, and Asia. There are 8,500 members, of which half are researchers and engineers. The society receives its basic budget from the government (DM 450 million in 1993); but most of its centers are for-profit organizations and receive two-thirds of their contracts from industry, including small- and medium-sized companies.

Yet another group of research institutions is the Blue List Institutions (*Wissenschaftsgemeinschaft Blaue Liste*). Like all independent research societies outside higher education, this group works cooperatively with universities, Fachhochschulen, industry, and ministries in the federal and state governments. The institutions belonging to this group also receive financial support of DM 1.2 billion from the federal and state governments. The Blue List Institutions include 82 institutions and have a membership of more than 10,000 individuals, of which about 5,000 are researchers.

CHAPTER THREE
ADMINISTRATION AND FINANCES

The organization of higher education institutions in Germany varies from state to state and sometimes within a state. Except for a few private universities, all higher education institutions are both public-law entities (*Körperschaften des öffentlichen Rechtes*) and state institutions. This means that each state has supervisory power and fiscal responsibility over the institution and that major regulations adopted by an institution need to be approved by the supervisory body of the state, usually the Ministry of Education and Cultural Affairs or the Ministry of Science and Research.

The states also approve examinations leading to advanced degrees and certifications for service to the public. In addition, state laws govern higher education budgets, personnel, buildings, and enrollments. The budgets of higher education institutions are allocated annually by the states, which have strict rules about how the funds can be spent.

The efficiency of having the state governments conduct planning for higher education institutions and detailing how funds are allocated has been called into question. It is argued that universities are complex institutions and that their expenses cannot be judged in state capitals. Some universities have proposed a global budget without spending designations in order to give the institutions more flexibility in using the funds and more autonomy for making related operational decisions.

The Federal Government and Higher Education

In the decades following World War II, as the number of institutions and their student population increased, it became necessary to coordinate how these institutions are governed throughout

tion of an institution, such as budget estimates and the distribution of personnel and material resources among the various departments. The senate also decides the number of students to be admitted, establishes departments and scientific units, and provides a forum for discussing basic issues concerning research, the promotion of scientists, examination regulations, and nominations to professorships. The duties of the two decision-making bodies are not always clear and can vary from institution to institution.

The organizational units of the institutions are the departments (*Fachbereiche*) or faculties (*Fakultäten*). Each department includes one large academic field or several smaller, related fields. The governing unit of the department is the department council. A professor always chairs the department council as the dean, although all of the groups who are represented in the university council also are represented in the department council.

Professors are civil servants and are paid accordingly. The commitments of a professor are to teaching, independent research, and guiding his or her department. A professor can be appointed only after fulfilling the basic requirements: finishing a course of study in higher education and demonstrating teaching aptitude and the ability to engage in academic or artistic activity. He or she needs to exhibit additional skills and knowledge through the process of *Habilitation*. In this process, the candidate shows off both his or her teaching ability and the ability to do independent research. The candidate defends a habilitation paper (*Habilitationsschrift*) in a public lecture and colloquium, with senior professors and peers as judges. When these steps have been taken and the results are successful, then the institution can recommend the candidate to the state authorities for appointment.

Other personnel involved in teaching are the senior assistants, senior engineers, and higher education lecturers (*Hochschuldozenten*). These positions are held by professionals who have passed the habilitation examination. In addition, teaching and research assignments are awarded to research assistants (*Wissenschaftliche Assistenten*), who have a doctoral degree but have not undertaken habilitation, and to research associates (*Wissenschaft-*

liche Mitarbeiter), who have completed their course of studies but do not have a doctorate. These people must be allowed time to do their own research to qualify for higher degrees and higher positions.

Usually, only the professors are employed on a permanent basis. The other teaching and research personnel are employed on a temporary basis with specific time limits in order to give more young people a chance to work in a research environment, to bring in fresh ideas, and to increase the number of potential teaching staff.

Other teaching staff may be employed to teach practical skills for which professorial qualifications are not necessary. Supplemental teaching assignments may be given to outsiders as temporary lecturers.

Planning and Financial Responsibility

Before unification, the number of West German students at institutions of higher education increased at a rapid rate; but there was no additional financial support for the institutions. After unification, the pressure for more places became even greater. The number of students in higher education rose from 900,000 in 1977 to 1.8 million in 1993, including more than 272,500 students from the former East Germany.

Even a drop in the birthrate of 2.5% in the late 1960s did not affect the growth in number of students, because there was a constant increase in the desire to attend higher education and because many students had to delay their studies. In 1991, only 800,000 study places were available for the 1.2 million prospective students who wanted to attend. Two million students are predicted to enroll by the turn of the century.

To stem the overflow of students into the universities, the rectors' conference of these institutions called for admissions restrictions (*numerus clausus*). In medicine, admissions restrictions already existed, and the rectors asked for extensions into such fields as computer science, economics, and law. However, the federal Minister of Science and Education rejected the imposition of admis-

33

sions restrictions because this provision is against the constitution. This position was confirmed by the German constitutional court when a case was brought before it.

One result of this increase in the student population has been an increase in the student-teacher ratio. In 1977 a university lecturer was responsible for 10 students; in 1991 a lecturer was responsible for 16 students. In the Fachhochschule the ratio was 1 to 33 in 1991. The Fachhochschulen currently are operating at 230% capacity, and admission restrictions are used for those schools. However, students who are unable to enroll in the Fachhochschulen enroll instead in the universities.

One solution is to increase the number of higher education facilities and expand existing institutions. However, 102,000 places need to be created just for the Fachhochschulen. That increase would cost DM 12 billion to 15 billion, and that amount is simply not available.

It has been a challenging task to plan for this increasing student population. Building new universities and expanding existing institutions are undertaken as joint ventures between the state and federal governments. However, while the states are supposed to pay half of the costs of these projects, their resources are insufficient; and the federal government has been required to contribute much more than its half of the costs.

Spending has increased at the federal level for university construction and in the states for staff and equipment. In 1991, the federal government provided DM 1.6 billion for expansion of facilities. In 1990 DM 4 billion were allocated to recruit more staff. DM 800 million are to be spent on the promotion of women. The goal is to recruit 25,000 more people over the next 10 years. The universities have been asked to recruit the best of their graduates for teaching and research, because many professors will retire soon. Thus the states have to provide money for material and staff.

The total cost of higher education from states' budgets, external funds, and administrative earnings in 1991 was DM 38.1 billion. Of this amount, 60% was spent on personnel, 27% on material, and 12% on buildings and large equipment. Not included in these costs is financial assistance paid to the students. In 1991, financial assistance to students was DM 3 billion.

Students pay no tuition. In addition, students in need receive financial assistance. Under the Federal Training Assistance Act (*Bundesausbildungsförderungsgesetz*), students can apply for financial assistance if their parents' income is low or if they can not support themselves. Sixty-five percent of this assistance is paid by the federal government; the states pay the rest. In addition, the states finance programs to assist students with housing and cost-of-living increases; and both the federal and state governments have set up programs for constructing student housing. Other areas of support are the gifted student programs and the foreign exchange programs for students and scholars.

In order to stay competitive in Europe and to increase the number of graduates, other measures also must be taken. For example, German industries complain about the length of study at the universities. In Germany, graduates start their working life at age 28; graduates in other countries start at about age 24 or 25. The average age of the first-year student in Germany is 22 years. This gives German students a disadvantage over foreigners in competing for positions.

CHAPTER FOUR
STUDENTS

In theory German students have free access to higher education. They pay no tuition and can apply for financial aid to meet their living expenses. They can choose the field of study and the institution they want to attend. However, in practice such open access comes only after clearing a number of hurdles; and an increasing number of students has made some restrictions and delays necessary.

Access to Higher Education

Most higher education students in Germany have attended the Gymnasium (secondary academic school) for nine or 10 years and have passed the final examination to obtain the Abitur or *Allgemeine Hochschulreife* (general right of entry to a higher education institution). The Abitur entitles the student to attend any university, Fachhochschule, or college of music or art.

The Gymnasium is the most common path to the Abitur. However, there are other ways for a student to achieve it. For example, a student can pass the Abitur in a specific subject area (the *Fachabitur* or *Fachgebundene Hochschulreife*), which restricts the student to a certain area of studies. To lift the restriction and achieve the Allgemeine Hochschulreife, the student must take an examination in a second foreign language. Also, persons who are gainfully employed can use the Second Chance Education (*Zweite Bildungsweg*) as an alternative path. They study in evening schools (*Abendschulen*), colleges, or other institutions to prepare for the Abitur.

About 91% of all students qualify for higher education by obtaining the Abitur, either as the culmination of their high school career or at some later time. But there also are a few other ways to qualify for higher education. For example, a student wanting to gain admission to a Fachhochschule can pass the final examination at a senior technical school, or *Fachoberschule*. He then achieves the *Fachhochschulreife*. Also, some states allow highly skilled workers to study in their specific field of expertise, provided they pass an entrance examination.

Recently, critics have challenged the validity of the Abitur as an entrance requirement. Since 1988 students in the upper level of the Gymnasium have been able to select subjects — such as psychology, sociology, economy, or information science — that traditionally have not been offered in the curriculum of the Gymnasium. Because some students no longer take the traditional core subjects — German, mathematics, foreign languages, and science — the critics suspect that students are tested in "soft" subjects and that the Abitur is no longer an indication of a student's aptitude for rigorous study in higher education.

The ministers of culture and education are under increasing pressure to revise the Abitur and to make the core subjects obligatory again. If no reform is accomplished, the University Rectors Conference is considering a general entrance examination. In addition, business is concerned about the quality of the Abitur and the subsequent studies of German students and believes that too many — currently 37% of students — take the exam.

All of this concern may be somewhat misplaced, as a variety of criteria in addition to the Abitur are used in admitting students:

- Length of time on the waiting list, gainful employment, or other special circumstances.
- Interviews conducted by the institutions.
- Students with special needs or foreign students.
- Test results.
- Previous subject-related training.
- Time spent in the military.

Even though the student has a right to study after admission standards have been met, and even though no entrance examinations are given at universities, this does not mean that the student always has a free choice. Certain popular courses of study have such a large number of applicants that admission restrictions need to be imposed. Admission to such popular courses as medical sciences, architecture, biology, psychology, business, and public administration is especially subject to restriction. A student may apply to the Central Office for Allocation of Study Places (ZVS) and request three locations in which to study one of these subjects; but the student will get his or her first choice only if the institution has a space. Overcrowding is so severe that in 1991-92, only 40,000 out of 100,000 applicants could be placed. Some institutions of higher learning impose their own restrictions because of overcrowding (Max-Planck-Institute 1994).

In this era particularly, one great concern is the access of women to higher education. Inequality in education in secondary schools was eliminated in the 1970s, and now slightly more women than men graduate from the Gymnasium. However, only 40% to 45% of the beginning university students are women. Several factors seem to play an important role: women seem to be less qualified than men, and adverse conditions in studies and poor employment prospects discourage them. At the Fachhochschulen, which have a more technical orientation, women make up only 30% of the enrollment. Likewise, the area of study makes a difference, of course. Beginning classes in engineering have only 12% women, whereas 70% of the beginning students in language arts and cultural studies are women. Tradition, role stereotypes, and real prospects for employment all play parts in this distribution.

The Path of Study

University and Fachhochschule studies have different purposes. Studies at the universities combine qualifications for a profession with academic qualifications, whereas studies at the Fachhoch-

41

schulen are geared more toward producing highly qualified practitioners.

At universities, students specialize in one subject or a combination of subjects. Studies are oriented to one subject and are designed to give students high skills and knowledge in a profession. Students do not have a general education requirement; instead, general education is part of the education received in secondary school.

A course of study in a German university lasts at least four years and ends with an examination. Earning a degree in medicine takes six years, and some teacher preparation courses take three years. After passing the exam, a student gets the degree that qualifies him or her to enter the profession. The student can go on to postgraduate studies, which can lead to the doctoral degree. There are few formalized curricula for doctoral studies; most are done on an individual basis. However, the concept of graduate colleges (*Graduiertenkollege*), in which the courses have a common structure, recently has been introduced.

Students working toward the first degree are usually full-time students; only the Correspondence University at Hagen offers enrollment on a part-time basis. Once enrolled in a university, the students have greater choices than Americans do in selecting classes and specializations within the chosen discipline. They can fulfill the requirements at their own pace and can supplement their studies with other classes. This is one reason why studies usually take longer than anticipated. Medicine and engineering are the exceptions; their time plan and sequence of courses is tightly structured.

Although the Federal Framework Act for Higher Education sets the period of study in the university at four years, students actually achieve the first degree in an average of six or more years. In addition, about 20% of the students change their specialization at some point and thus prolong their stay at the university (Max-Planck-Institute 1994). In law the prescribed time is about three and a half years; it actually takes six or more years. Only achieving a degree for being a teacher in the lower grades takes less than four years.

The academic year is divided into a winter and a summer semester. University students attend classes for a total of 28 weeks in a year; Fachhochschule students attend for 36 weeks. The course of study usually consists of two segments. The beginning segment, or basic studies (*Grundstudium*), lasts about two years and provides a general foundation in a subject. It concludes with an intermediate examination (*Zwischenprüfung*) or a preliminary degree examination (*Diplomvorprüfung*).

The Grundstudium is followed by the second segment, which is roughly equivalent to a major field concentration in a U.S. university. This is called main studies, or *Hauptstudium*. The Hauptstudium gives the students specialized, in-depth knowledge in a field. The student can choose his or her own focus for study by selecting courses from a group of compulsory subjects (*Wahlpflichtfächer*) and optional subjects (*Wahlfächer*). No cumulative credits are earned over the course of study as in American institutions.

The Hauptstudium also concludes with an examination. Depending on the subject studied or the profession chosen, this final examination can be a university examination in form of a *Diplomprüfung* (degree examination) or *Magisterprüfung* (master's examination) or it could be a state or an ecclesiastical examination. Some professions require a student to take both a state examination and a university examination. The university examination usually requires a major paper or thesis, as well as written and oral examinations.

The Magisterprüfung can be taken in many fields, such as linguistics and cultural studies, the social sciences, economics, foreign language, and the sciences. The academic title is *Magister Artium,* or Master of Arts. The Diplomprüfung usually is taken in the natural sciences, engineering, economics, and social sciences. The degrees are awarded according to the particular subject studied, such as *Diplom-Chemiker* or *Diplom-Engenieur*.

State examinations are regulated by the state, a federal agency, or both. State examinations are taken by aspiring professionals in teaching, law, medicine, dentistry, veterinary medicine, pharmacy, and food chemistry. Aspiring clergy conclude their theological studies with an examination sponsored and controlled by the church.

Studies at the Fachhochschule are shorter and more structured than at the university. The subject areas correspond in part to the ones at the university, but the emphasis is on practicality. The suggested study time is usually three and a half to four years and includes one or two semesters for practical experiences in addition to academic training. If students come from previous training programs or apprenticeships, they may be exempted from the practical semesters. Even so, studies at the Fachhochschule also usually extend beyond four years.

The studies at the Fachhochschule also are divided into Grundstudium and Hauptstudium. As in the university, the Grundstudium concludes with a preliminary examination, and the Hauptstudium culminates in a final examination, which includes a long research paper, several written examinations, and an oral examination. The examination is oriented toward the practical, with problems taken from the field. After having successfully completed the examination, the candidate is awarded an academic title according to the discipline, such as *Diplom-Ingenieur*. Fachhochschule students can achieve a degree in 18 disciplines, which have about 40 specialties. Most of the programs are in engineering, including architecture, civil engineering, ceramics, soil conservation, steel construction, textiles, and many others.

Student Profile

The great majority of students in higher education come from families in which the parents also had higher education. Only 6% of the students come from working-class families. This socioeconomic distribution of students was the impetus for earlier reforms; and since the 1960s, when fewer students had access to higher education, the social, economic, and educational background of the students has greatly changed (Wissenschaftsrat 1993).

Because they need the income, some students take on professional activities during their studies. This is especially true for more advanced students, who usually seek employment when other sources of financing are no longer available or when they wish to better their standard of living, for example, by purchasing a car. The students' need to work often allows them to study only part time.

Students vary in their levels of involvement with their institutions. Germany does not have a tradition of the university campus as a center for students' social lives. Thus some students spend their free time away from the institution. Others, however, are very much involved in the university's social life; they study and spend their free time around the institutions.

While a student can enter higher education at the age of 19, most entering students at the universities are about 21.6 years old; at the Fachhochschulen most entering students are 23.2 years old. One reason for this late start is that many students work or engage in vocational training before starting higher education. In addition, some students have to fulfill their obligation of 12 months military service or 15 months alternative service before they can enroll in higher education. This late start and the long study periods bring the average age of the graduating student to 28.8 years at universities and 27.3 years at the Fachhochschulen (Preisert and Framhein 1994).

Each year about 70,000 students drop out, some just before the final examination. The reasons these dropouts give are varied, but many claim the overfilled lecture halls, impersonal teaching, and bad counseling influenced their decision ("Beruf: Studienabbrecher," 1995). Others fear the transition to the working world, and some are afraid of the final examination. These students are encouraged to get counseling from the institution and from the local office of human development (*Arbeitsamt*).

Chronic housing shortages also make it hard for students to find reasonably priced places to live. Students stay with their parents when that is possible, but only about 23% of university students and 34% of Fachhochschulen students are able to do so. Most students rent apartments, either alone or with other students. Only 10% of the students in the former West German states reside in residence halls. In the former East Germany, 60% live in residence halls.

Residence halls are administered by the Student Welfare Service (*Studentenwerk*). Each institution has a Studentenwerk, which is part of the federally subsidized German Student Welfare Service (*Deutsches Studentenwerk*). The Studentenwerk represents the students' interest in political and social issues and administers the institution's dining facilities and health services. Students are required to pay a mandatory fee for the organization and for health and accident insurance.

Students also pay a mandatory fee to belong to the General Student Committee (*Allgemeiner Studentenausschuß*, or *ASTA*). This committee is administered by students and charged with academic, social, and cultural matters. Generally, the students' main concerns are to participate in academic counseling, to help establish teaching content and examination regulations, to formulate social issues at the institution, and to influence institutional politics (Preisert and Framhein 1994, p. 109).

At this writing, however, most students in higher education are showing little or no interest in institutional politics. For example, recent activities against the proposed imposition of interest for subsidy loans did not draw large crowds of protesters. And even though all the political parties have student groups, very few students participate. This was not always the case.

Financial Aid

Although there is no tuition for higher education in Germany, the students are responsible for their living expenses. Some students qualify for financial assistance under the government's Federal Training Assistance Act (*Bundesausbildungsförderungsgesetz*, or *BAföG*), which is administered by the Studentenwerk. The BAföG is a loan that provides only supplementary income.

The BAföG is granted only for the federally determined standard period of study, which in most cases is four years, though in some cases it can be extended for 12 months if the student can

46

prove progress toward an examination. In addition, beginning in the student's fourth semester, this financial assistance depends on the student's performance.

In 1995 about 437,000 students, or about 27%, received BAföG subsidies (Preisert and Framhein 1994, p. 106). The maximum allowance under the BAföG is DM 1,050 per month, but very few students receive this amount. Most students depend on other sources of income. In 1995, for example, more than two-thirds of students were employed.

Initiated in 1971, the BAföG originally was a grant to students. In 1983 it became an interest-free loan that could be paid back in 25 years after graduation. But in 1995 the federal government decided to charge regular interest rates on the loan. That change in the terms of the BAföG loan has been controversial. Equality of opportunity is a very sensitive issue in Germany, but the new BAföG terms mean that students from lower income levels will no longer have an equal chance of enrolling in higher education. Student leaders fear the new arrangement will lead to admission restrictions by social class, in which only students who have the financial backing of their parents will be allowed to enroll.

In addition to the BAföG loans, scholarships are available for exceptionally talented students. For example, the Federal Ministry of Education and Science awards scholarships to exceptionally talented students and doctoral candidates. In 1993, this and several other organizations provided almost DM 110 million in funds for the gifted. Some states provide additional funds for exceptional students; and private foundations, unions, and churches provide stipends and loans for students at both the universities and Fachhochschulen.

Employment Prospects

Until the mid-1970s, graduates from higher education institutions were almost always guaranteed employment. There were not many graduates, and the demand for these qualified professionals was high.

When the academic secondary schools were opened to a larger population, access to higher education increased as well. Already in the 1960s, great concern was voiced over the increase in graduates, and a fear of a possible "intellectual proletariat" was discussed, meaning that too many young people would graduate without a job. However, until the 1970s, the job market was able to absorb an additional 2.5 million graduates.

Beginning in 1975, there was a constant increase in unemployment for graduates; from 30,000 in 1975 to 140,000 in 1988, easing slightly to about 110,000 in 1991. One problem has been that about half of the graduates were employed in the public service sector, and tighter budgets have caused the federal and state governments to limit employment. Thus graduates have had to rely more on the private sector.

However, the job market for higher education graduates has always been better than for the average employee. In the last 25 years, graduates have become more than 10% of the labor force. In addition, it is predicted that a majority of graduates with civil service jobs will retire after 1995. New areas of employment are opening in the public sector, including environment, waste management, and energy planning. One factor affecting public sector employment is that, though the civil service has its own Fachhochschulen, graduates from these institutions are less likely to advance into upper-level management than are the graduates of the universities.

The private sector has increased its hiring of graduates because it now needs highly qualified professionals in places where such qualifications were not needed before. Industry prefers graduates from Fachhochschulen, because these graduates are highly qualified practitioners in the fields of engineering and business administration. They have the skills needed for planning and managing the ever-increasing complexity of industry. Graduates even accept positions in industry for which they are overqualified in order to have prospects for advancement.

CHAPTER FIVE

TEACHER EDUCATION

Teacher education in Germany is known for being thorough and highly academic. It is conducted in two parts, the first at universities for theory and the second in state-run seminars for induction into teaching. However, even with the practical induction, teacher training still is considered too theoretical. Thus there have been calls for a better balance between theory and practice. In addition, the various types of schools in Germany seem to call for different teaching qualifications, which also need to be addressed in teacher training programs.

The Structure of Teacher Education

Although teacher qualifications earned in any state are recognized throughout Germany, the path to becoming a teacher differs somewhat from state to state. Teacher training in the largest and most populous state, North Rhine-Westphalia (*Nordrhein-Westfalen*), provides a representative example. Most of the following discussion is based on that state's system.

The Abitur or its equivalent is the prerequisite for entering into a teacher training program. The program is divided into two phases. The first consists of studies at a university or a college of art or music. The second phase, an introduction to school practice, takes place in study seminars and specially designated schools and is sponsored by the state, rather than by a university.

Teacher certification and assignment is divided according to grade level and school type:

- Teaching certification for the primary level allows teaching in primary school grades 1-4.
- Teaching certification for the secondary level I allows teaching in grade levels 5-10 at a main school (Hauptschule), middle school, academic secondary school, and comprehensive school.
- Teaching certification for the secondary level II allows teaching at the upper level of the Gymnasium, the comprehensive school for grades 11-13, and the vocational school.
- Special education certification allows teaching at multi-level special education schools grades 1-10 and at regular schools that incorporate special education.

The first phase of teacher training, the time spent at the university, differs in length depending on the grade level. For the primary level and secondary level I, the length of study is six semesters; for secondary level II and special education, it is eight semesters. In addition, it should take one semester to prepare for the examination. However, in practice, students very seldom finish in the prescribed time of six or eight semesters and take the examination one semester later.

The second phase of teacher training, the introduction to school practice, takes two years regardless of the level at which the student plans to teach.

The studies at the university also are divided into two parts. The first focuses on basic and main studies, and the second focuses more on subject matter than on pedagogical science.

Basic studies comprise the fundamentals of subject matter, didactics, pedagogy, and related subjects. An interim examination is given that shows the student's success at this level and his or her aptitude for further studies. The main studies build on the basics by expanding and deepening subject matter, didactics, and pedagogic theories. After the student moves to the second half of his or her university studies, subject-matter studies occupy most of the student's time, with only 18% to 20% of the time for pedagogy. More time is spent on pedagogy by those who are seeking certification for the lower levels of education; thus pedagogy occupies 25% of the studies for those seeking certification at the primary level and secondary level I.

Part of the student's pedagogical studies include practical experiences at a school. Students have the opportunity to observe instruction and to plan, teach, and analyze lessons with the help of a mentor in an actual school setting. Through this experience, they can explore their aptitude or willingness to enter the teaching profession. This practical experience usually is scheduled during semester breaks, and it does not exceed eight weeks.

For those students who will teach at the primary level, the obligatory courses are pedagogy, German, and mathematics. Students also have to choose one extra subject from the following: art, music, sports, textile design, social studies, or science/technology. The prospective teacher must take 42 hours per semester in a major subject, 21 hours in each of the other two subjects, and 28 hours in pedagogy, for a total of 112 hours per semester.

Secondary level I teachers are required to study two subjects for 42 hours per semester each and pedagogy for 28 hours per semester. The combination of subjects can vary greatly.

For the secondary level II, even more combinations are possible, depending on the qualification the student seeks or the school type at which he or she would like to teach. All must take 30 hours per semester in pedagogy and didactics and 120 hours in subject matter. The student wishing to teach at the Gymnasium or Gesamtschule selects two subjects he or she would like to teach. For vocational schools or comprehensive schools, students can select one subject and one vocationally oriented area, such as economics, to achieve a teaching qualification. A student also can qualify for vocational school teaching by selecting two subjects in the vocational area with one special area.

To become a special education teacher, a student can choose a combination of a regular subject and a vocational subject or a combination of a subject for the primary level and one for the secondary level for a total of 40 hours per semester. He or she also needs 30 hours per semester in regular pedagogy and 80 hours in special education and rehabilitation.

Many other combinations are possible. In addition, the student can pass extra examinations to qualify to teach across grade levels. This is encouraged especially for teachers at the Gymnasium, but teachers with multiple qualifications can be found at all schools.

After having completed the studies at the university, the student is eligible to apply for the first state examination. This examination consists of three sections:

- A written scientific investigation in the subjects studied (except for primary and secondary level I, where more emphasis is placed on pedagogical areas).
- A written examination under supervision in the teaching subjects and pedagogical sciences. Each section of this written examination will take about four hours.
- An oral examination of up to 40 minutes, dealing with problem solving in the area of studies.

The successful candidate then can apply for the second phase of teacher preparation, conducted at special study seminars and in specially designated schools controlled by the education authority of each state. This two-year phase is supposed to bridge the gap between the theoretical university studies and the practical demands of teaching and advising.

The seminars explore the application of pedagogy and didactics, as well as school law and school administration, for three hours each week. Two hours each week are spent in seminars on subject matter, where practical applications in the chosen subjects are explored.

Selected training schools are connected to the seminars. At these schools, the candidate observes and teaches 12 hours a week under supervision and counseling by a mentor in the chosen and related subjects. Up to four hours of unsupervised teaching are allowed. In addition, seminar instructors visit the candidate at regular intervals. Both mentors and seminar instructors give constant feedback, both written and oral, on the candidate's progress. At the end of the first year, the candidate receives a grade, which is used only for information purposes.

In the second year, the candidate continues supervised teaching while also preparing for the second state examination. This examination consists of a written paper, prepared over a three-month period, dealing with the demonstration, analysis, and solution of a problem or issue related to school practice and teaching. The candidate also must demonstrate his or her teaching ability during an official teaching session observed by an examination committee. An oral examination of 60 minutes dealing with subject matter studied in the seminars brings the second phase of teacher training to an end.

The teacher candidate is provisionally employed during this training phase and thus has some earnings. However, passing the final examination does not guarantee further employment. Employment depends on possible job openings and is subject to economic and sociopolitical conditions.

Inservice Education

Many teachers volunteer to continue and update their training. The subjects most often taken are pedagogy, psychology, sociology, and didactics. Recently, environmental studies, media, and information science have been added to the list of subjects that teachers can study. In addition, the state and federal governments offer many courses in government and political issues, and private enterprises also sponsor advanced training for teachers.

Inservice training can take place at the university, regional training centers, or at the school. It usually takes place during school hours; and teachers can be excused for days or even weeks to receive intensive training, update their skills and knowledge, or gain further teaching qualifications.

On average, each teacher takes part in inservice training at least once a year. Some participate more than once a year, others not at all (Führ 1989). There is no connection between salary and additional training unless a teacher qualifies for a different level of teaching.

Theoretical versus Practical Training

Studies at German universities focus on theory without concern for practice in a chosen profession. The only exceptions are law and medicine, which are oriented strongly toward practice. Many critics have questioned the usefulness of this theoretical orientation for professions in general, and especially for teacher education (Flach 1994).

Germany's current teacher training process has its origin in the last century, when Gymnasium teachers were trained at the university. The assumption was that good scientists and scholars would be good teachers, though they received no training in teaching. Eventually, future teachers were required to study pedagogy, including didactics, psychology of learning, and related subjects. However, these were taught as purely academic subjects with little concern for practical application.

In contrast to those who would teach in the Gymnasium, those who intended to teach in elementary schools and what is now called the *Hauptschule* (main school) were trained at teacher seminars, not at universities. In some areas, students could enter teacher seminars as soon as they graduated from the Hauptschule, and they were trained very much as apprentices were trained. However, by the beginning of this century, autonomous teacher colleges were established (Führ 1989). And in the 1970s and 1980s these teacher colleges were incorporated into the universities. As the training of these teachers was upgraded, it became even more academic and theoretical.

The problem of focusing too strongly on theory was supposed to be solved through the second phase of teacher preparation, which was created to provide a contrast to the academic studies. However, the second phase of teacher training actually reinforces the theoretical approach of university studies. Not only are the teacher candidates steeped in theory, but the mentors and instructors at the training seminars and schools seem to be concerned more about theoretical approaches than about practical applications.

This approach no longer seems to be suitable for teaching the growing number of diverse students who are attending the Gymnasium and Realschule. Until the early 1960s, only 15% of an age cohort qualified to attend the Gymnasium, and another

20% qualified for the Realschule. Now 30% of an age cohort enroll in the Gymnasium, and even more enroll in the Realschule. These schools have become institutions for mass education, but teacher training has not responded to these new needs.

One suggestion for reform is to adopt the teacher training system that was used in the former German Democratic Republic (GDR) before unification. Teacher training programs in the GDR were conducted in teacher colleges for secondary schools or institutes for teacher training for primary schools. The training concentrated on broad, streamlined aspects of subject matter and the transmission of the technical skills of teaching. In addition, the time it took to complete teacher training was shorter in the GDR, and students could begin teacher training at an earlier age than in West Germany (Max-Planck-Institute 1994).

The positive aspects of teacher training in the GDR were its practical approach and that teachers, scientists, and the education bureaucracy worked together to prepare teachers in an integrated training program. However, it also was centrally organized and included political and ideological indoctrination. From the West German point of view, teacher training in the GDR was too restrictive and deprived students of their self-determination (Kirchhöfer 1994).

Unfortunately, this system was abandoned after unification. Many critics have suggested that Germany missed its chance to reform teacher education when it abandoned the system used in the GDR (Rust 1994; Kirchhöfer 1994).

Teacher Training and the European Union

In the next few years the European countries are to be integrated. This will have severe consequences for teacher education in Germany.

Almost all European countries have their own model of education, and teacher education varies from country to country. In addition, Germany does not have a completely uniform training system; rather, it has a federal system with common goals and similar overall structures, but with varying systems among the states.

In the European Union, teacher education will be integrated across Europe, which means that teachers will be able to choose the country in which they would like to teach, and their qualifications must be accepted in that country. Teachers would need to have the same rights and privileges in every country. Thus a teacher from Spain could become a civil servant in Germany with the same retirement and health benefits. However, teacher training in Spain differs in goals, structure, and length of study from teacher training in Germany. Therein, of course, lie many problems.

German teachers will be at a disadvantage because of the years of preparation they must undergo. For example, teacher training in France ends at a minimum age of 23. In Germany the minimum age is 26 if a student follows the officially prescribed number of semesters of study — and few German students finish their university studies in that time. Thus most German teachers can start at about age 28 to 30. For male teachers an additional year of military or public service prolongs the entrance to professional life.

It remains to be seen if the European countries can find a solution to this problem. First, the various European countries need to agree on what is a good and efficient teacher training system. The main issue will be how the education systems and teacher education can be compared and readjusted to meet the needs of a united Europe.

Which way teacher training in Germany will go is uncertain. However, the constant debate and the forces influencing the system from within the profession and from the new developing social order seem certain to bring a change.

CHAPTER SIX

FUTURE DIRECTIONS

Many critics complain about the slowness or complete absence of change in German higher education. Yet others claim that higher education has shown great adaptability over the years, particularly in the effort to make higher education more accessible. Both views are partly correct. Higher education in Germany *has* changed over time; and it still is changing to meet the demands of German society, its students, and the economy. But more needs to be done, and some things need to be done rather quickly. The ever-increasing number of students, the unification of Germany, and the European Union are just a few of the issues that must be addressed in the future.

Some Recommendations

The Science Council (*Wissenschaftsrat*) is the main force in planning and recommending changes. It bases its recommendations on thorough research, and most of its recommendations are followed.

According to the Wissenschaftsrat, spending must be increased for higher education in order to accommodate the greater numbers of students and to meet growing demands for more highly educated professionals with practical knowledge. Because the number of students in higher education has outgrown the capacity of higher education facilities, the facilities need to be expanded and upgraded. For example, although education at a Fachhochschule is less expensive and more efficient than at a university, only one-third of the total student population in Germany attends and graduates from Fachhochschulen because of enrollment restrictions. Expanding the system of Fachhochschulen would allow these schools to lift their enrollment restrictions, which in turn would ease the universities' enrollment burden.

In addition, Fachhochschulen need to expand their subject offerings from only technical, commercial, and administrative subjects to others that currently are found only at universities, such as law, medicine, languages, business administration, applied natural sciences, and the training of vocational teachers. This would make the Fachhochschulen more attractive to a greater variety of students.

Universities also need to offer a more differentiated program of study for their students. That might involve establishing a program with shorter and more focused courses that would allow the majority of students to enter a profession after they have achieved the diploma or master's degree. The traditional program still would be provided for those students who wish to study for a position in research and teaching in higher education. The students with the shorter curriculum would ease the crowding at the university by leaving earlier, and they would enter the world of work at an age more comparable to that of students in other European countries.

Another way to ease enrollment restrictions is to replace the Abitur with a series of subject-specific qualifying examinations. It no longer is possible to allow every young person who passes the Abitur to enter the university and develop an individual study plan for personal fulfillment. If students were restricted to studying in areas in which they qualified through an examination, their courses of study would be streamlined and there would be more spaces available for other students. However, students fear that such a system would place their academic freedom in jeopardy.

Fachhochschulen and universities also should establish cooperative programs to make the Fachhochschulen more attractive for beginning students. Students who successfully finish their study at a Fachhochschule would be allowed to continue their education at a university without first having to pass an additional examination. This arrangement also would add another dimension to basic research, because Fachhochschule graduates would bring practical experience to their research.

Yet another way to ease the enrollment burden is to expand opportunities for part-time study, which currently is very limited. Professional academies (*Berufsakademien*) already provide a form of part-time study, and eventually they could gain full recognition as part of higher education. However, if part-time study were extended to the Fachhochschulen and the universities, it would make attending these institutions more feasible for many students. In addition, part-time study would allow professionals to update their skills and acquire new qualifications.

As lifelong education and flexible learning become increasingly important to Germany's economy, distance learning also will gain in importance. Those higher education institutions that are not yet involved in distance learning should be encouraged to participate. Depending on the kind of study pursued, a student may be asked to pay a fee for the service.

Change and Autonomy

Higher education institutions are not free to manage their own affairs, and they are dependent on detailed budget allocations by the states. The state is responsible for higher education and exercises that right rather rigorously, not only in financial areas but also in regulating examinations and courses of study. Thus the institutions have little incentive for change.

Higher education institutions also do not need to compete for students, because there are more students looking for a place in higher education than the institutions currently can accommodate. And because no mechanism exists to evaluate or rank teaching and research, all institutions are thought to have the same quality; a degree received from one institution is as valid — and as valued — as a degree from any other.

If higher education reform is to be successful, it has to come from the institutions themselves. Reform requires greater autonomy and decision-making authority at the institutional level. But the various proposals for reform are debated widely, with many critics expressing the fear that reform could cause a drop in the quality of these institutions.

One proposal would make higher education institutions more responsible for their own governance and funds. The states still would finance these institutions, but the detailed allocation of funds would be made by each institution's senate. The institutions also would be responsible for hiring teaching staff and recruiting students.

In addition, an evaluation system would be used to tie the financing of these institutions to their proven achievement and the needs that develop out of their accomplishments. The universities and Fachhochschulen would compete for funds based on their performance in teaching. Research funding already is allocated mostly on the basis of competition. However, no baseline for such evaluations currently exists, although the German Rectors' Conference has initiated a pilot program at several universities. This proposal is intended to give the universities and Fachhochschulen an incentive to plan and to budget efficiently.

For some critics, this proposal does not go far enough. They argue that government-run institutions, such as railroads and postal services, are being privatized. Since privatization works for other German institutions, this also should be tried with institutions of higher education. The government, these critics argue, should get out of higher education altogether and allow these institutions to become free, financially and legally independent institutions (Schily 1994).

Tradition as a Barrier to Change

One significant barrier to reform has been tradition. Those institutions that have attempted to adopt nontraditional approaches have faced difficulties. For example, Europa-University Viadrina, a new university in Frankfurt an der Oder, close to the Polish border, attempted to break with traditional course offerings and merge many subjects under the title of Cultural Studies (*Kultur-*

wissenschaften). This area was to include economics, law, foreign language, and the humanities. However, the approach was not accepted in its original form, and a watered-down approach had to be tried. Indeed, the concept remains under debate even in its milder form (Weiler 1994).

Another nontraditional aspect of this university is its international approach. It draws students from nearby Poland, and it also would like to attract an international faculty. However, employment status and payment to foreign professionals is different than for domestic faculty. There is very little incentive for foreign faculty to do the same work as German faculty without getting equal pay or benefits. Unless this issue is resolved, universities and Fachhochschulen will not be able to attract foreign scientists and researchers on a permanent basis (Weiler 1994).

Another aspect of tradition is that each university must offer all subjects in order to be fully recognized. Thus there is little difference between universities. The negative effects of this sameness were demonstrated at a new university that was established in Potsdam after unification. Potsdam is the capital of Brandenburg, the state that surrounds Berlin; and the two cities are close to each other. Berlin already had three well-established universities, and the new university had the same traditional course offerings as the Berlin universities. Because many students preferred to study these subjects in nearby Berlin, the new university had to close some of its departments for lack of students (Jung 1995).

Another issue is the age of those teaching in higher education. The average age of a university professor is 51.7 years; in the Fachhochschule, it is 50 years. Between 1996 and 2005, half of all professors will retire; however, many positions may go unfilled (as they already do) because of lack of money. Older professors are set in their ways and have little incentive to change. And the younger professors are not in a position to bring about change because they are few in number and still have to earn their tenure.

Many critics had hoped that unification would provide a chance for innovation. New institutions could be founded that provided special course offerings, and all higher education institutions could coordinate their programs in order to avoid unnecessary duplication. But the opportunity provided by unification could not overcome tradition, and many critics now believe that the chance to renew higher education in Germany has been missed.

Germany and the European Community

The European Community will bring more challenges to German higher education. Because all citizens of the European Community will have the freedom to move and work within the member countries, their educational qualifications need to be recognized by all the member countries. However, member countries have different education systems with differing content and length of study. Because job qualifications need to be comparable, all the countries need to develop education systems that meet common standards.

According to the Maastricht Treaty of 1993, the European Community respects member countries' responsibility for education. There are no rules as far as content and organization of education systems is concerned. The recognition of diplomas and examinations is based on the mutual trust that the education received is equivalent in quality and content throughout the member states.

The European Community intends to supplement educational efforts in the various countries, not replace them. Furthermore, it intends to promote a European dimension in education through language teaching and encouraging the mobility of students and teachers. This would include mutual recognition of diplomas, time of study, and achievement of students. Any course of study three years or more in length is recognized throughout the union. Other areas promoted by the union are cooperation between education institutions, exchanges of information and experiences, and the development of distance education.

One complication the European Community presents to German higher education concerns the federated structure of Germany, in which each of the 16 states is responsible for education and culture. Thus a teacher from Italy cannot simply apply to one federal agency for employment but must deal with the different laws and rules of the various states. In addition, the restrictive civil service law, which was mentioned earlier, will present obstacles to foreign teachers who want permanent employment and benefits in Germany (Thomas 1996*a*). One result of these conflicts may be that the carefully guarded educational authority of the states, already altered by the Framework Act for Higher Education, will be further eroded.

The Maastricht Treaties also gave the European Community increased powers in education through financial support for various programs for schools, vocational training, and foreign language teaching. For example, in the 1995/96 academic year, about 160,000 students and 1,700 institutions participated in the ERASMUS Program. This program promotes cooperation and foreign study for all students up to the doctorate. It also includes exchange of higher education personnel.

The ERASMUS Program is now part of SOCRATES, a program that includes all levels education, as well as foreign language assistance for students. SOCRATES has a budget of DM 1.6 billion for five years. More than half of that budget is used for cooperation in higher education and student exchange programs (Thomas 1996*b*). The long-range goal is for 10% or more of students to study abroad for a semester. In 1995 about 6% of the students took advantage of this opportunity, and about 22,000 universities participated in this program. The German Academic Exchange Service is the national information center for student exchanges.

The European Community realizes the need to stay competitive in research and technology; therefore it provides assistance especially for information technology, environmental research, biotechnology, biomedical research, transport, and socioeconomic research. Financial support is given to cooperative projects between partners from different countries. Partners can be independent research institutions, universities, or industrial research projects.

Despite these trends, Europe still seems to be a long way from having a united education system. The cultural sovereignty of member countries makes it difficult to acknowledge degrees from other countries and to allow foreign professionals to practice in one's country (Mohr 1996). While degrees are officially accepted and the European Community has laws and agreements that promote free movement of people and free practice of a learned profession, national safeguards and fear of competition slow this process. The nations still try to protect their citizens from other countries' "dominance." However, eventually there will be unity in this area.

The European Community is moving to consolidate efforts and unite for a better future for its citizens. No great results have been achieved yet, but the continuing process is most important.

REFERENCES

"Beruf: Studienabbrecher." *Süddeutsche Zeitung*, 2 December 1995.

Brubacher, John, and Rudy, Willis. *Higher Education in Transition*. New York: Harper & Row, 1968.

Flach, Herbert. "Lehrerbildung Zwischen Wissenschaftsorientierung und Berufsbezogenheit. Historische Entwicklung und Aktuelle Probleme." *Lehrerbildung im Vereinigten Deutschland* (DIPF/Kr.) . Frankfurt am Main: Land, 1994.

Framework Act for Higher Education. Bonn: Federal Ministry of Education and Science, 1994.

Führ, Christoph. *Schools and Institutions of Higher Education in the Federal Republic of Germany: A Survey of Educational Policy and the Educational System*. Bonn: Inter Nationes, 1989.

Führ, Christopher. "The German University — Basically Healthy or Rotten: Reflections on an Overdue Reorientation of German Higher Education Policy." Trans. from German. *European Education* 25 (Winter 1993-94).

"Hochschulen: Letzte Hoffnung." *Der Spiegel* 24 (June 1996). http://www.spiegel.de/archiv/index.html

Jung, Joachim. "Ein Umbau nach Verblichenen Plänen." *Süddeutsche Zeitung*, 14 October 1995.

Kirchhöfer, Dieter. "Lehrerbildung in den neuen Bundesländern im Spannungsfeld von Deutscher und Europäischer Integration." In *Current Changes and Challenges in European Teacher Education*, edited by Theodor Sander. Bruxelles: Reseau d'Institutions de Formation, 1994.

Max-Planck-Gesellschaft. "Zur Förderung der Wissenschaften ist die Nachfolgerin der 1911 gegründeten." Internet: http://www.rzg.mpg.de/mpg.html, 24 January 1996.

Max-Planck-Institute für Bildungsforschung. *Das Bildungswesen in der Bundesrepublik Deutschland: Structuren und Entwicklungen im Uberblick*. Hamburg: Rowolt Taschenbuch Verlag, 1994.

Mohr, Brigitte. "Europe as an Educational Community." *Bildung und Wissenschaft* 1 (1996): 14-15.

Perspectiven für Wissenschaft und Forschung auf dem Weg zur Deutschen Einheit: Zwölf Empfehlungen. Köln: Wissenschaftsrat, 1990.

Preisert, Hansgert, and Framhein, Gerhild. *Higher Education in Germany*. Bonn: Federal Ministry of Education and Science, 1994.

Rust, Val D. "Die Deutsche Vereinigung — neue Chancen für die Lehrerbildung?" *Bildung und Erziehung* 2 (1994).

Schily, Konrad. "Unabhängige Universitäten in einer freien Gesellschaft." *Politik und Zeitgeschichte* 25 (1994): 35-38.

Stifterverband für die Deutsche Wissenschaft, Wozu Universitäten-Universitäten wohin? Essen: Verwaltungsgesellschaft für Wissenschaftspflege, 1993.

Thomas, Volker. "Reform of EU Education Policy: New Programs to Provide Greater Mobility." *Bildung und Wissenschaft* 1 (1996): 4-7. a

Thomas, Volker. "Living in Europe, Working for Europe: An Overview of the European Union's Education Programmes." *Bildung und Wissenschaft* 1 (1996): 8-9. b

Weiler, Hans. "Conceptions of Knowledge and Institutional Realities: Reflections on the Creation of a New University in Eastern Germany." Paper presented at the Annual Meeting of the Comparative and International Education Society, San Diego, 21-24 March 1994.

Wissenschaftsrat. *10 Thesen zur Hochschulpolitik*. Berlin, 1993.

Internet Addresses

Arbeitsgemeinschaft der Großforschungseinrichtungen. Internet: http://www.verwaltung.unimainz.de/Dezl/forschungsfoerderung/db-stift/arb7.html.

Der Spiegel. Internet: http://www.spiegel.de/archiv/index.html.

Fraunhofer Gesellschaft. Internet: http://www.fhg.de/contact.html,.

Wissenschaftsgemeinschaft Blaue Liste. Internet: http://www.fizchemie.de/wbl/inhalt.html.

ABOUT THE AUTHOR

Hans G. Lingens is an adjunct professor in the School of Education at California Lutheran University, where he teaches social foundations of education, comparative education, and research methods. His primary research area is in comparative education and teacher training. He also is the editor of *European Education*.

Lingens grew up in Germany and attended the University of Cologne. He holds a B.S., M.A., and Ed.D. from the University of Southern California. For 25 years, he worked in the Los Angeles Unified School District. He taught a variety of subjects in high school, including biology, chemistry, German, and history; and he served for five years in the district's office for research and evaluation. Lingens also has taught at the University of Southern California and at Mount Saint Mary's College.